The Little Black Book of
Marriage Wisdom

Quotes on Weddings, Divorce,
& Happily Ever After

Mike Kowis, Esq.

THE LITTLE BLACK BOOK OF
MARRIAGE WISDOM:
Quotes on Weddings, Divorce, & Happily Ever After
by Mike Kowis, Esq.

Copyright © 2024 Mike Kowis, Esq.

All rights reserved. No part of this book may be reproduced or transmitted in any form or by any means, electronic or mechanical, including photocopying, recording, or by any information storage and retrieval system, without the written permission of the publisher except where permitted by law.

DISCLAIMER NOTICE: The quotes contained in this book are intended for educational and entertainment purposes only. No warranties of any kind are expressed or implied. By reading this book, the reader acknowledges that the author and publisher are not engaged in the rendering of tax, legal, or financial advice and further agrees that under no circumstances is the author or publisher responsible for any losses, direct or indirect, which are incurred as a result of the use of the information contained in this book, including, but not limited to, errors, omissions, or inaccuracies.

Library of Congress Control Number: 2024912423

ISBN-13: 979-8-9900133-6-0 (paperback)

ISBN-13: 979-8-9900133-5-3 (eBook)

www.mikekowis.com

Lecture PRO Publishing

Conroe, Texas

Dedication

This book is dedicated to my lovely bride of 26 years and counting. To reward Jessica for faithfully standing by my side all these years, I offer my sincerest gratitude plus this "priceless" dedication. As if that's not enough, I'll also throw in a lifetime supply of terrible dad jokes. You're welcome.

Love you, babe!

Testimonials

Here's what people are saying about *The Little Black Book of Marriage Wisdom*:

> **You won't find anyone disappointed with *The Little Black Book of Marriage Wisdom*... unless they actually read it.**
> – *Mike's life coach*

> **What does Mike know about weddings? He thought Holy Matrimony was an 80s punk rock band.** – *Mike's couples therapist*

> **Another book of quotes? Hard to tell if Mr. Kowis ran out of words or just got lazy.** – *Mike's publicist*

> **I'm not saying Mike is old, but he put the AGE in MARRIAGE.** – *Mike's chiropractor*

> **Mike is to marriage advice what J. Lo is to marriage advice.**
> – *Mike's mother-in-law*

> **The title of this book contains the word "little," but that's not the only thing tiny about Mike.** – *Mike's podiatrist*

> **Mike would make a great marriage counselor. He's always spouting off helpful statistics like marriage is the number one cause of divorce.** – *Mike's mailman*

> ***The Little Black Book of Marriage Wisdom* is the PERFECT book to bring along on a couples camping trip... you never know when you'll run out of toilet paper!** – *Mike's sassy sister*

But seriously, you're gonna enjoy the following collection of amusing marriage quotes. Let's just hope they are more engaging than the silly testimonials above!

Contents

Dedication iii
Testimonials v
Introduction 1
Chapter 1: Famous Sayings 5
Chapter 2: Wisecracks 11
Chapter 3: The Big Day 25
Chapter 4: Wedding Toasts 29
Chapter 5: By Definition 35
Chapter 6: True Love 43
Chapter 7: Til Death Do Us Part 53
Chapter 8: Best Friends 55
Chapter 9: Success 59
Chapter 10: Anniversaries 63
Chapter 11: Never! 67
Chapter 12: Divorce 73
Chapter 13: Religious Teachings 85
Chapter 14: Happily Ever After 99
Chapter 15: Miscellaneous 105
Conclusion 117
Let's Get Connected 123
Acknowledgements 125
About The Author 127

INTRODUCTION

> A successful marriage requires falling in love
> many times, always with the same person.
> – *Mignon McLaughlin*

Photo Courtesy of Little Chapel of Hearts (Las Vegas)

Jessica and I renewed our vows a few years ago at one of those cheesy wedding chapels in Vegas. Honestly, I was not looking forward to this overpriced, 20-minute ceremony hosted by an Elvis impersonator. To my surprise, we smiled and giggled during the entire event and it turned out to be the highlight of our fabulous trip! Celebrating 25 years of marriage that weekend gave me a chance to reflect on how lucky I am to share my life with the one person I can't live without. If you are looking for a fun and memorable way to renew your wedding vows, I highly recommend going to one of the wedding chapels in Vegas.

This momentous occasion also made me think deeply about the exclusive, long-term commitment between two people in love commonly known as marriage. What is it really and why is it so important? Is it just an ingenious marketing campaign devised by the wedding industry or is there a profound reason why couples are so eager to tie the knot? Are there any spiritual or religious teachings about this special relationship? Why do some people fear holy matrimony? More important, what causes so many marriages to end in divorce while others go the distance? We all grapple with these burning questions from time to time. To anyone contemplating the institution of marriage and what it means to say "I do," take heart! You might find some of the answers in this silly book filled with 519 humorous and thought-provoking quotes about weddings, divorce, and happily ever after.

The quotations below touch on a wide variety of concepts related to marriage, including well-known sayings, jokes, marriage advice, the wedding ceremony, religious teachings, divorce, and much more. Each chapter covers a different topic, but there is a degree of overlap.

Following this Introduction, Chapters 1 and 2 include famous sayings and humorous quotes, respectively. In addition to Chapter 2, you'll find funny quips sprinkled throughout the entire book.

Next, Chapters 3 and 4 discuss the wedding day and what to say when raising a glass in honor of the newlyweds, respectively. Chapter 5 explores the true meaning of marriage.

Chapters 6, 7, and 8 each cover a common characteristic found in all lasting marriages: love, commitment, and friendship, respectively. Chapter 9 shares successful marriage tips, and Chapter 10 gives observations about wedding anniversaries.

On a darker note, Chapters 11 and 12 describe the notion that marriage is never a good option and share a variety of viewpoints on divorce, respectively.

To wrap things up, Chapter 13 provides spiritual teachings about the sacred bond of holy matrimony, Chapter 14 covers happiness in marriage, and Chapter 15 includes sayings that didn't fit neatly elsewhere. Finally, the Conclusion distills the following quotations into a handful of salient points and shares my top ten list.

I hope you enjoy the following marriage quotes as much as I enjoyed gathering them. Happy reading – and you can quote me on that!

CHAPTER 1

Famous Sayings

> **Happy wife, happy life.**
> *– Unknown*

I love being married. It's so great to find that one special person you want to annoy for the rest of your life.

— *Rita Rudner*

When you realize you want to spend the rest of your life with somebody, you want the rest of your life to start as soon as possible.

— *When Harry Met Sally (1989 film)*

Marriage is like a deck of cards. In the beginning, all you need is two hearts and a diamond. By the end, you wish you had a club and a spade.

— *Unknown*

I'm selfish, impatient, and a little insecure. I make mistakes, I am out of control, and at times hard to handle. But if you can't handle me at my worst, then you sure as hell don't deserve me at my best.

– *Marilyn Monroe*

Look, you want to know what marriage is really like? Fine. You wake up, she's there. You come back from work, she's there. You fall asleep, she's there. You eat dinner, she's there. You know? I mean, I know that sounds like a bad thing, but it's not.

– *Everybody Loves Raymond (1996-2005 TV series)*

My most brilliant achievement was my ability to be able to persuade my wife to marry me.

– *British Prime Minister Winston Churchill*

Come, let's be a comfortable couple and take care of each other! How glad we shall be that we have somebody we are fond of always, to talk to and sit with.

– *Charles Dickens*

There is nothing nobler or more admirable than when two people who see eye-to-eye keep house as man and wife, confounding their enemies and delighting their friends.

– *Homer, The Odyssey (701)*

If I get married, I want to be very married.

— *Audrey Hepburn*

When I said I would die a bachelor, I did not think I should live till I were married.

— *William Shakespeare, Much Ado About Nothing (1598)*

When a man says to me, "Let us work together in the great cause you have undertaken, and let me be your companion and aid, for I admire you more than I have ever admired any other woman," then I shall say, "I am yours truly;" but he must ask me to be his equal, not his slave.

— *Susan B. Anthony*

It takes six years to learn to live together and get over the most furious fits of wishing you hadn't married him, and hating him, but after that he becomes a habit and a property and you stop bothering about it.

— *George Bernard Shaw*

We all have a childhood dream that when there is love, everything goes like silk, but the reality is that marriage requires a lot of compromise.

— *Raquel Welch*

Say you'll marry me when I come back or, before God, I won't go. I'll stay around here and play a guitar under your window every night and sing at the top of my voice and compromise you, so you'll have to marry me to save your reputation.

– *Margaret Mitchell, Gone with the Wind (1936)*

A lady's imagination is very rapid; it jumps from admiration to love, from love to matrimony, in a moment.

– *Jane Austen, Pride and Prejudice (1813)*

Marriage is neither heaven nor hell, it is simply purgatory.

– *President Abraham Lincoln*

My wife and I tried to breakfast together, but we had to stop or our marriage would have been wrecked.

– *British Prime Minister Winston Churchill*

A girl can wait for the right man to come along, but in the meantime that doesn't mean she can't have a wonderful time with all the wrong ones.

– *Cher*

I first learned the concepts of non-violence in my marriage.

– *Mahatma Gandhi*

A young man married is a man that's marred.

— *William Shakespeare, All's Well That Ends Well (1604)*

People say, "Jeez, it must be hard to stay married in show business." I think it's hard to stay married anywhere. But if you marry the right person, it might work out. We give each other a natural sense of support for whatever the other wants to pursue. Our marriage doesn't require vast work.

— *Tom Hanks*

After all these years, I see that I was mistaken about Eve in the beginning; it is better to live outside the Garden with her than inside it without her.

— *Mark Twain, The Diaries of Adam & Eve: Translated by Mark Twain (1906)*

You don't marry the person you can live with – you marry the person you can't live without.

— *Unknown*

CHAPTER 2

Wisecracks

> "I am" is reportedly the shortest sentence in the English language. Could it be that "I do" is the longest sentence?
> – *George Carlin*

I've been in love with the same woman for forty-one years. If my wife finds out, she'll kill me.

– *Henny Youngman*

All men make mistakes, but married men find out about them sooner.

– *Red Skelton*

Before you marry a person, you should first make them use a computer with slow internet to see who they really are.

– *Will Ferrell*

Married men live longer than single men. But married men are a lot more willing to die.

– *Johnny Carson*

Men who have a pierced ear are better prepared for marriage – they've experienced pain and bought jewelry.

– *Rita Rudner*

I was married by a judge. I should have asked for a jury.

– *Groucho Marx*

Keep your eyes wide open before marriage, half shut afterwards.

– *U.S. Founding Father Benjamin Franklin*

Bachelors have consciences, married men have wives.

– *Samuel Johnson*

Marriage is about the most expensive way for the average man to get laundry done.

– *Burt Reynolds*

Well, sure, the vows say "in sickness and health" and "for better or worse" and all that, but that's kind of like clicking okay to the terms and conditions when you download an app or sign up for a credit card. You don't think any of that is going to apply to you.

– Lori Gottlieb, Maybe You Should Talk to Someone (2019)

My wife has a slight impediment in her speech. Every now and then she stops to breathe.

– Jimmy Durante

What's it like? Being married?

Cold feet. Middle of the night you're sleeping, suddenly, wham, you've got ice cold feet warming themselves on the back of your legs.

– Alan Brennert, Moloka'I (2003)

Bride, n. - A woman with a fine prospect of happiness behind her.

– Ambrose Bierce, The Unabridged Devil's Dictionary (1911)

It's tough to stay married. My wife kisses the dog on the lips, yet she won't drink from my glass.

– Rodney Dangerfield

The trouble with wedlock is that there's not enough wed and too much lock.

– *Christopher Morley*

Marriage is give and take. You'd better give it to her or she'll take it anyway.

– *Joey Adams*

When you see what some girls marry, you realize how they must hate to work for a living.

– *Helen Rowland, A Guide To Men: Being Encore Reflections Of A Bachelor Girl (2007)*

I do not think you can name many great inventions that have been made by married men.

– *Nikola Tesla*

If you think that your partner has been cheating, then take a look at their will. If a past lover is in there, then it is probable that some form of infidelity has occurred.

– *Steven Magee*

Whatever you may look like, marry a man your own age – as your beauty fades, so will his eyesight.

– *Phyllis Diller*

After fourteen years of matrimony, I have discovered that hoping your other half telepathically reads your mind only leads to someone wanting to punch the other one in the face.

– *Twinkle Khanna, Mrs Funnybones: She's just like You and a lot like Me (2015)*

There is one thing more exasperating than a wife who can cook and won't, and that's a wife who can't cook and will.

– *Robert Frost*

To me, most Indian weddings seemed like time travel. The groom arrives on a horse, departs in a car.

– *Daksh Tyagi, Tripping Abroad (2022)*

We either say "I do," or we say "aideu" – for good.

– *Erik Forrest Jackson, Muppets Meet the Classics: The Phantom of the Opera (2017)*

A good wife always forgives her husband when she's wrong.

– *Milton Berle*

I believe people ought to mate for life… like pigeons or Catholics.

– *Woody Allen, Manhattan (1979)*

By all means, marry. If you get a good wife, you'll become happy. If you get a bad one, you'll become a philosopher.

– *Socrates*

Instead of getting married again, I'm going to find a woman I don't like and give her a house.

– *Lewis Grizzard*

I don't think my wife likes me very much, when I had a heart attack she wrote for an ambulance.

– *Frank Carson*

Whenever you want to marry someone, go have lunch with his ex-wife.

– *Shelley Winters*

Marriage: A word which should be pronounced "mirage."

– *Herbert Spencer*

A bride at her second marriage does not wear a veil. She wants to see what she is getting.

— *Helen Rowland*

Many women get married to practice taking care of a baby before having one of their own.

— *George Hammond*

Paying alimony is like feeding hay to a dead horse.

— *Groucho Marx*

Bachelors know more about women than married men; if they didn't, they'd be married too.

— *H.L. Mencken*

Marriage is nature's way of keeping us from fighting with strangers.

— *Alan King*

Personally, I know nothing about sex because I have always been married.

— *Zsa Zsa Gabor*

Marriage has no guarantees. If that's what you're looking for, go live with a car battery.

– *Erma Bombeck*

There is nothing like a knowledge of farming and an acquaintance with the habits of domestic animals to teach a man how to manage his wife.

– *W. Somerset Maugham, Mrs Craddock (1902)*

12% of people marry because they are completely in love. 88% of people marry just so they are then liable for only half of their rent.

– *Mokokoma Mokhonoana*

Marriage is like the Middle East, isn't it? There's no solution.

– *Willy Russell, Shirley Valentine (1986)*

Not only is love blind, it's a little hard of hearing.

– *Brian P. Cleary, You Oughta Know By Now (2010)*

Finding a life partner is like choosing a bed. You need one as a friend either in times of health or sickness. Freshness or weariness. Happiness or sadness. And we can be certain that we've picked the right one without having to sleep with it first.

– *Isman H. Suryaman*

Bigamy is having one wife too many. Monogamy is the same.

– *Oscar Wilde*

When your wife asks you for your opinion, she doesn't really want your opinion. She wants her opinion – just in a deeper voice.

– *T. Rafael Cimino, The Heir Apparent (2014)*

Husband secretly lowers the thermostat, and I secretly turn it back up. We both vehemently deny touching it. Marriage is fun.

– *Stephanie Ortiz*

Taking up marriage is a good excuse for taking up cursing. These is my words.

– *Nancey E. Turner*

A man wants too many things before marriage, but only peace after it.

– *Pawan Mishra, Coinman: An Untold Conspiracy (2015)*

"What nonsense people talk about happy marriages!," exclaimed Lord Henry. "A man can be happy with any woman, as long as he does not love her."

– *Oscar Wilde, The Picture of Dorian Gray (1890)*

When a man steals your wife, there is no better revenge than to let him keep her.

– *Sacha Guitry*

I married for love, but the obvious side benefit of having someone around to find my glasses cannot be ignored.

– *Cameron Esposito*

A man in love is incomplete until he has married. Then he's finished.

– *Zsa Zsa Gabor*

After 45 years of marriage, when I have an argument with my wife, if we don't agree, we do what she wants. But, when we agree, we do what I want!

– *Jacques Pepin*

I married beneath me. All women do.

– *British Parliament Member Nancy Astor*

Marriage is the triumph of imagination over intelligence. Second marriage is the triumph of hope over experience.

– *Oscar Wilde*

Maybe the difference between first marriage and second marriage is that the second time at least you know you are gambling.

— *Elizabeth Gilbert, Committed: A Skeptic Makes Peace with Marriage (2009)*

Every culture has some ritual for joining two people together and making them stay that way, and ours is giving tax breaks.

— *Bauvard, Some Inspiration for the Overenthusiastic (2011)*

You know there is a name for people who are always wrong about everything all the time… Husband!

— *Bill Maher*

Some people claim that marriage interferes with romance. There's no doubt about it. Anytime you have a romance, your wife is bound to interfere.

— *Groucho Marx*

There is a correlation between the number of days since a man last had sex and the number of things that he is willing to do for a woman.

— *Mokokoma Mokhonoana*

The desire to get married is a basic and primal instinct in women. It's followed by another basic and primal instinct: the desire to be single again.

– *Nora Ephron*

As you get older, you've probably noticed that you tend to forget things. You'll be talking with somebody at a party, and you'll know that you know this person, but no matter how hard you try, you can't remember his or her name. This can be very embarrassing, especially if he or she turns out to be your spouse.

– *Dave Barry*

When two people are under the influence of the most violent, most insane, most delusive, and most transient of passions, they are required to swear that they will remain in that excited, abnormal, and exhausting condition continuously until death do them part.

– *George Bernard Shaw, Getting Married (1908)*

Love is a lot like a backache. It doesn't show up on x-rays, but you know it's there.

– *George Burns*

Spend a few minutes a day really listening to your spouse. No matter how stupid his problems sound to you.

– *Megan Mullally*

The man may be the head of the household. But the woman is the neck, and she can turn the head whichever way she pleases.

– *Nia Vardalos*

Women who marry early are often overly enamored of the kind of man who looks great in wedding pictures and passes the maid of honor his telephone number.

– *Anna Quindlen*

The best way to get most husbands to do something is to suggest that perhaps they're too old to do it.

– *Ann Bancroft*

He held up his index finger. Rule one: in any dispute between mates, the male is always to blame, even when he is clearly blameless. Rule two – his middle finger joined the first – whenever in doubt, refer to rule one.

– *C.L. Wilson, Lord of the Fading Lands (2007)*

The trouble with some women is that they get all excited about nothing – and then marry him.

– *Cher*

Someone told me the delightful story of the crusader who put a chastity belt on his wife and gave the key to his best friend for safekeeping, in case of his death. He had ridden only a few miles away when his friend, riding hard, caught up with him, saying "You gave me the wrong key!"

– *Anais Nin*

Do you know what it means to come home at night to a woman who'll give you a little love, a little affection, a little tenderness? It means you're in the wrong house, that's what it means.

– *Henny Youngman*

CHAPTER 3

The Big Day

> **Wedding: the point at which a man stops toasting a woman and begins roasting her.**
> *– Helen Rowland*

Many people spend more time planning the wedding than they do in planning the marriage.

– *Zig Ziglar*

There is no correlation between how much money was spent on the wedding and how long the marriage is going to last.

– *Mokokoma Mokhonoana*

Let's be honest. Half of all wedding celebrations are a lot like cheering for the frickin' Titanic on the day of departure.

– *Vindy Teja*

The music at a wedding procession always reminds me of the music of soldiers going into battle.

— *Heinrich Heine*

A wedding band is the smallest handcuff ever made. I'm glad I chose my cellmate wisely.

— *Unknown*

The most dangerous food is wedding cake.

— *James Thurber*

Oh! How many torments lie in the small circle of a wedding ring!

— *Colley Cibber, The Double Gallant (1707)*

I think a lot of people who feel as though they desperately want to be married oftentimes simply desperately want to have a wedding.

— *Elizabeth Gilbert*

Saw a wedding in the church. It was strange to see what delight we married people have to see these poor fools decoyed into our condition.

— *British Parliament Member Samuel Pepys*

I think a lot of people get so obsessed with the wedding and the expense of the wedding that they miss out on what the real purpose is. It's not about a production number, it's about a meaningful moment between two people that's witnessed by people that they actually really know and care about.

– *Jane Seymour*

CHAPTER 4

Wedding Toasts

> **Don't ever stop dating your wife and don't ever stop flirting with your husband.**
> *– Unknown*

People are meant to go through life two by two. 'Tain't natural to be lonesome.
  – *Thornton Wilder, Our Town (1938)*

To keep your marriage brimming with love in the wedding cup, whenever you're wrong, admit it; whenever you're right, shut up.
  – *Ogden Nash*

You are my strength. You are my reason. The beginning that ends my journey alone.
  – *Clodagh O, planned to PERFRECTION (2022)*

What a terrifyingly beautiful thought that you are the beginning of forever. I love you, and life for me has just begun.

    – Kamand Kojouri

The first to apologize is the bravest.
The first to forgive is the strongest.
The first to forget is the happiest.

    – Unknown

The bride and groom – may their joys be as bright as the morning, and their sorrows but shadows that fade in the sunlight of love.

    – Minna Thomas Antrim

Marriage hath in it less of beauty, but more of safety than the single life; it hath more care, but less danger, it is more merry, and more sad; it is fuller of sorrows, and fuller of joys; it lies under more burdens, but it is supported by all the strengths of love and charity, and those burdens are delightful.

    – Bishop Jeremy Taylor

Marriage stands the test of times when both you and your spouse work towards making things better. And we are tested the most when we face adversities. If you can sail through the adversities as one, as a team, then you have won half the battle.

    – Unknown

What greater thing is there for two human souls then to feel that they are joined for life – to strengthen each other in all labor, to rest on each other in all sorrow, to minister to each other in silent, unspeakable memories at the moment of the last parting?

– *George Eliot*

I pray that my days will be long at your side. Let me fill and satisfy every longing in your soul. May your hand be in mine, by sun and by night. Let our breaths twine and our blood become one, until our bones return to dust. Even then, may I find your soul still sworn to mine.

– *Rebecca Ross*

Marriage may appear as the culmination of adventure to some people, but to me, it is the dawn of an extraordinary odyssey. It is the genesis of an epic journey, where two souls unite to conquer life's grandest challenges hand in hand. So you know what? Embrace it as the thrilling prologue to a story filled with passion, devotion, and boundless love, where every day promises a new chapter of breathtaking adventures together.

– *Emmanuel Apetsi*

When someone is the song to your heart's rhythm, dance with them through the swings of life.

– *James and D'Leene DeBoer*

Be sweet to one another. Stay in this beauty and brawl against the world's power of pulling apart. Recall Old Testament terminology: covenant, sacred, sacrifice. And mind always that Adam wasn't a schlep fruitily duped by Eve. He turned his back on God because he knew that a paradise without her was no paradise at all.

– *William Giraldi, Busy Monsters (2011)*

Let there be spaces in your togetherness and let the winds of the heavens dance between you. Love one another but not make a bond of love: Let it be rather a moving sea between the shores of your souls.

– *Kahlil Gibran, The Prophet (1923)*

What really matters is that he will love you, that he will respect you, that he will honor you, that he will be absolutely true to you, that he will give you the freedom of expression and let you fly in the development of your own talents. He is not going to be perfect, but if he is kind and thoughtful, if he knows how to work and earn a living, if he is honest and full of faith, the chances are you will not go wrong, that you will be immensely happy.

– *Gordon B. Hinckley*

Two hearts in love need no words.

– *Marceline Desbordes-Valmore*

Life is too short to be anything but happy. So, kiss slowly. Love deeply. Forgive quickly. Take chances and never have regrets. Forget the past, but remember what it taught you.

– *Abhishek Shukla, KISS Life: Life Is What You Make It (2018)*

I think of how each person in a marriage owes it to the other to find individual happiness, even in a shared life. That this is the only way to grow together, instead of apart.

– *Emily Giffin, Heart of the Matter (2010)*

Compromise, communicate, and never go to bed angry – the three pieces of advice gifted and regifted to all newlyweds.

– *Gillian Flynn, Gone Girl (2012)*

CHAPTER 5

By Definition

> **Marriage is like trading in the adoration
> of many for the sarcasm of one.**
> – Mae West

This is what marriage really means: helping one another to reach the full status of being persons, responsible beings who do not run away from life.

– *Paul Tournier*

Marriage is when women finally get what they want, and men wave the white flag, unaware of the firing squad that awaits them.

– *Jack Freestone*

Marriage …the most advanced form of warfare in the modern world.

– *Malcolm Bradbury, The History Man (1975)*

Marriage is more about snore strips and flannel nightgowns than candlelight dinners.

— Barbara Bartlein, *Why Did I Marry You Anyway?: Overcoming the Myths That Hinder a Happy Marriage* (2003)

Marriage is like a game of chess. Except the board is flowing water, the pieces are made of smoke, and no move you make will have any effect on the outcome.

— Jerry Seinfeld

Marriage is one sweet way in which one can taste heaven on earth. Similarly, I can also become hell on earth.

— Israelmore Ayivor

Marriage is either a winning lottery ticket or a straitjacket.

— Alice Feeney, *Rock Paper Scissors* (2021)

Marriage is an attempt to solve problems together which you didn't even have when you were on your own.

— Eddie Cantor

Marriage is a wonderful invention; but then again so is a bicycle repair kit.

— Billy Connolly

Marriage is a fine institution, but I'm not ready for an institution.

– *Mae West*

Marriage is like a tripod where two legs represent the husband and wife, and the third leg represents the respect between them.

– *Sukant Ratnakar, Quantraz (2021)*

Marriage is supposed to be a union between two equals who love and support each other, not a master-slave relationship in which the man commands a docile woman.

– *Robert Thier, Storm and Silence (2016)*

Marriage is not the end of romance, it is the beginning. They know that they have years in which to deepen their connection, to experiment, to regress, and even to fail. They see their relationship as something alive and ongoing, not a fait accompli. It's a story that they are writing together, one with many chapters, and neither partner knows how it will end. There's always a place they haven't gone yet, always something about the other still to be discovered.

– *Esther Perel, Mating in Captivity: Reconciling the Erotic and the Domestic (2006)*

Marriage is not kick-boxing, it's salsa dancing.

– *Amit Kalantri*

Marriage is a partnership, not a democracy.

– *Nicholas Sparks, The Best of Me (2010)*

For marriage is like life in this – that it is a field of battle, and not a bed of roses.

– *Robert Louis Stevenson*

Marriage is a mosaic you build with your spouse. Millions of tiny moments that create your love story.

– *Jennifer Smith*

Marriage – a book of which the first chapter is written in poetry and the remaining chapters in prose.

– *Beverley Nichols*

Marriage is the only adventure open to the cowardly.

– *Voltaire*

Marriage: a hopeful, generous, infinitely kind gamble taken by two people who don't know yet who they are or who the other might be, binding themselves to a future they cannot conceive of and have carefully omitted to investigate.

– *Alain de Botton, The Course of Love (2016)*

Marriage is the mother of the world. It preserves kingdoms, and fills cities and churches, and heaven itself.

— *Bishop Jeremy Taylor*

Marriage is the beginning of an everlasting melody of love.

— *Debasish Mridha*

Marriage is a workshop where the husband works and the wife shops.

— *Unknown*

Marriage is like watching the color of leaves in the fall; ever changing and more stunningly beautiful with each passing day.

— *Fawn Weaver*

Marriage is one long sacrifice.

— *Edith Wharton, The Age of Innocence (1920)*

Matrimony is a serious thing.

— *Anne Brontë, The Tenant of Wildfell Hall (1848)*

Marriage is the union of two I's to form a V. Both I's have to tilt equally to make a good V. I's standing tall can never make a V.

— *Ashok Kallarakkal*

Marriage is like a fingerprint. Everyone's is different.

— *Angela Lam Turpin*

Marriage thrives as a union of two givers, not a balance between a giver and a taker.

— *Dr. Lucas D. Shallua*

In marriage, everyday you love and everyday you forgive. It is an ongoing sacrament, love and forgiveness.

— *Bill Moyers*

A long marriage is two people trying to dance a duet and two solos at the same time.

— *Anne Taylor Fleming*

Marriage is not a ritual or an end. It is a long, intricate, intimate dance together and nothing matters more than your own sense of balance and your choice of partner.

— *Amy Bloom*

Marriage is in countless cases a failed attempt to resuscitate a relationship.

— *Mokokoma Mokhonoana*

Marriage is popular because it combines the maximum of temptation with the maximum of opportunity.

— *George Bernard Shaw*

Marriage is a partnership, not a corporate venture.

— *Sophie Page, To Marry a Prince (2011)*

Marriage is about compromise; it's about doing something for the other person, even when you don't want to.

— *Nicholas Sparks, The Wedding (2003)*

Marriage is a garden that requires two gardeners to care for it.

— *Nate Hamon*

Marriage is like a well-built porch. If one of the two posts leans too much, the porch collapses. So each must be strong enough to stand on its own.

— *Deb Caletti, The Secret Life of Prince Charming (2009)*

Marriage isn't about winning. It's about lasting.

— *Mark Gorman*

Marriage is like vitamins: we supplement each other's minimum daily requirements.

— *Kathy Mohnke*

CHAPTER 6

True Love

> **True love begins when nothing is looked for in return.**
> *– Antoine de Saint-Exupéry*

You know you're in love when you can't fall asleep because reality is finally better than your dreams.

– Dr. Seuss

I long for the day when someone loves me as much as women in commercials love yogurt.

– Kevin Molesworth, The Rudman Conjecture on Quantum Entanglement (2021)

Love seems the swiftest, but it is the slowest of all growths. No man or woman really knows what perfect love is until they have been married a quarter of a century.

– Mark Twain

You don't love someone for their looks, or their clothes, or for their fancy car, but because they sing a song only you can hear.

— *Oscar Wilde*

The only way love can last a lifetime is if it's unconditional. The truth is this: love is not determined by the one being loved, but rather by the one choosing to love.

— *Stephen Kendrick, The Love Dare (2008)*

I love you, not only for what you are, but for what I am when I am with you. I love you, not only for what you have made of yourself, but for what you are making of me.

— *Roy Croft*

You know you are in love when the two of you can go grocery shopping together.

— *Woody Harrelson*

I've tried so many times to think of a new way to say it, and it's still I love you.

— *Zelda Fitzgerald*

Love doesn't mean a state of perfect caring. To love someone is to strive to accept that person exactly the way he or she is, right here and now – and to go on caring through joyful times and through times that may bring us pain.

— *Fred Rogers, Dear Mister Rogers, Does It Ever Rain in Your Neighborhood?: Letters to Mister Rogers (1996)*

To love your spouse is to love yourself.

— *Tiffany Majors, Drop the Hustle (2020)*

We're all a little weird. And life is a little weird. And when we find someone whose weirdness is compatible with ours, we join up with them and fall into mutually satisfying weirdness – and call it love – true love.

— *Robert Fulghum*

Love is more about being the right person than finding the right person.

— *Barbara Bartlein, Why Did I Marry You Anyway?: Overcoming the Myths That Hinder a Happy Marriage (2003)*

Where there is love, there is life.

— *Mahatma Gandhi*

True love is not something you find, true love is something you nurture together.

– *Abhijit Naskar, Visvavatan: 100 Demilitarization Sonnets (2024)*

Whenever you keep score in love, you lose.

– *Kamand Kojouri*

We loved with a love that was more than love.

– *Edgar Allen Poe*

Love of a husband and wife is an endless journey without a destination, but the journey itself is the goal – let us embrace the journey and cherish every moment so that love lasts a lifetime.

– *Mozammel Khan*

The best and most beautiful things in this world cannot be seen or even heard, but must be felt with the heart.

– *Helen Keller*

There's a big difference between falling in love with someone and falling in love with someone and getting married. Usually, after you get married, you fall in love with the person even more.

– *Dave Grohl*

Tis better to have loved and lost than never to have loved at all.

– *Lord Alfred Tennyson*

Love recognizes no barriers. It jumps hurdles, leaps fences, penetrates walls to arrive at its destination full of hope.

– *Maya Angelou*

"I love you more than I hate everything else.

– *Rainbow Rowell, Landline (2014)*

Love is an act of endless forgiveness; a tender look which becomes a habit.

– *Peter Ustinov*

When love scratches the heart and tickles the brain nothing can impede its onward journey.

– *Dennis Adonis III*

If I know what love is, it is because of you.

– *Hermann Hasse*

There must be a stronger foundation than mere friendship or sexual attraction. Unconditional love, agape love, will not be swayed by time or circumstances.

— *Stephen Kendrick, The Love Dare (2008)*

To love and be loved is to feel the sun from both sides.

— *David Viscott*

Love isn't a state of perfect caring. It is an active noun like struggle. To love someone is to strive to accept that person exactly the way he or she is, right here and now.

— *Fred Rogers*

If I had a flower for every time I thought of you, I could walk through my garden forever.

— *Alfred Tennyson*

Being deeply loved by someone gives you strength, while loving someone deeply gives you courage.

— *Lao Tzu*

Romantic love is ecstasy and intoxication, but marriage is a long voyage.

— *Kosho Uchiyama, The Zen Teaching of Homeless Kodo (1981)*

Love without truth is sentimentality; it supports and affirms us but keeps us in denial about our flaws. Truth without love is harshness; it gives us information but in such a way that we cannot really hear it.

– Timothy Keller, *The Meaning of Marriage: Facing the Complexities of Commitment with the Wisdom of God* (2011)

The way I feel about him is like a heartbeat – soft and persistent, underlying everything.

– Becky Albertalli

Love is giving up control. It's surrendering the desire to control the other person. The two – love and controlling power over the other person – are mutually exclusive. If we are serious about loving someone, we have to surrender all the desires within us to manipulate the relationship.

– Rob Bell, *Sex God: Exploring the Endless Connections Between Sexuality and Spirituality* (2007)

Your absence has not taught me to be alone, it merely has shown that when together we cast a single shadow on the wall.

– Doug Fetherling

True love stories never have endings.

– Richard Bach

Lots of people want to ride with you in the limo, but what you want is someone who will take the bus with you when the limo breaks down.

– Oprah Winfrey

When you trip over love, it is easy to get up. But when you fall in love, it is impossible to stand again.

– Albert Einstein

Who, being loved, is poor?

– Oscar Wilde

But we loved with a love that was more than love.

– Edgar Allen Poe

Love's about finding the one person who makes your heart complete. Who makes you a better person than you ever dreamed you could be. It's about looking in the eyes of your wife and knowing all the way to your bones that she's simply the best person you've ever known.

– Julia Quinn, *The Viscount Who Loved Me* (1814)

Love doesn't just sit there, like a stone, it has to be made, like bread; remade all the time, made new.

– Ursula K. LeGuin, *The Lathe of Heaven* (1971)

The power of vulnerability is also truly magic. Vulnerability, I've become convinced, is the way to get love. And, of course, many of us decide not to be vulnerable because we're afraid. But vulnerability is the way to get love, romantic or otherwise.

– *Cheryl Strayed*

The art of love…is largely the art of persistence.

– *Albert Ellis*

To be fully seen by somebody then and be loved anyhow – this is a human offering that can border on miraculous.

– *Elizabeth Gilbert, Committed: A Skeptic Makes Peace with Marriage (2009)*

Love does not consist of gazing at each other, but in looking outward together in the same direction.

– *Antoine de Saint-Exupéry*

If you love 'em in the morning with their eyes full of crust; if you love 'em at night with their hair full of rollers, chances are, you're in love.

– *Miles Davis*

Love is a temporary madness. It erupts like volcanoes and then subsides. And when it subsides, you have to make a decision. You have to work out whether your roots have so entwined together that it is inconceivable that you should ever part. Because this is what love is.

– *Louis de Bernières*

CHAPTER 7

Til Death Do Us Part

> **Love is not maximum emotion. Love is maximum commitment.**
> – *Dr. Sinclair Ferguson*

I am a very committed wife. And I should be committed, too – for being married so many times.

– *Elizabeth Taylor*

When women hold off from marrying men, we call it independence. When men hold off from marrying women, we call it fear of commitment.

– *Warren Farrell*

Monogamy is not considered natural. Humans are designed to be promiscuous, but we choose to be faithful to our partners. It is a choice that is done out of true commitment… love.

– *L.A. Nettles, Butterflies (2022)*

The hard truth is that love isn't always what sustains our commitment, but it is our commitment that sustains love.

    – Cindy David, *What it Means When I Say "I Do"* (2023)

If you both care for each other more than you care for yourself, your marriage will endure all.

    – Lisa Tawn Bergren

A marriage should start with a strong foundation and a gift to symbolize his commitment.

    – Elizabeth Camden, *Carved in Stone* (2021)

Great marriages don't happen by luck or by accident. They are the result of a consistent investment of time, thoughtfulness, forgiveness, affection, prayer, mutual respect, and a rock-solid commitment between a husband and a wife.

    – Dave Willis

CHAPTER 8

Best Friends

> **Marriage, ultimately, is the practice of becoming passionate friends.**
> *– Harville Hendrix*

Marriage is sharing your life with your best friend, enjoying the journey along the way, and arriving at every destination together.

– Fawn Weaver

If there is such a thing as a good marriage, it is because it resembles friendship rather than love.

– Michel de Montaigne

Love is like a friendship caught on fire. In the beginning a flame, very pretty, often hot and fierce, but still only light and flickering. As love grows older, our hearts mature and our love becomes as coals, deep-burning and unquenchable.

– Bruce Lee

The essence of marriage is companionship, and the woman you face across the coffee urn every morning for ninety-nine years must be both able to appreciate your jokes and to sympathize with your aspirations.

— *Elbert Hubbard*

The key to a successful and lasting marriage relationship is friendship.

— *Manuel Corazzari*

Never marry a person who is not a friend of your excitement.

— *Nathaniel Branden, The Psychology of Romantic Love (2000)*

Love is a friendship set to music.

— *Joseph Campbell*

Marriage is the highest state of friendship. If happy, it lessens our cares by dividing them, at the same time that it doubles our pleasures by mutual participation.

— *Samuel Richardson*

It is not a lack of love, but a lack of friendship that makes unhappy marriages.

— *Friedrich Nietzsche*

Make sure you marry someone who laughs at the same things you do.

— *J.D. Salinger*

We're friends, too. We love each other, but we actually like each other—and that's an important distinction there. Love is passion and all of that stuff, but actually liking somebody and enjoying someone's company is something slightly different, and it lasts longer. So you can have both, and I think that's important. Be married to your best friend.

— *Sting*

When marrying, ask yourself this question: Do you believe that you will be able to converse well with this person into your old age? Everything else in marriage is transitory.

— *Friedrich Nietzsche*

Happy is the man who finds a true friend, and far happier is he who finds that true friend in his wife.

— *Franz Schubert*

CHAPTER 9

Success

> **A perfect marriage is just two imperfect people
> who refuse to give up on each other.**
> *– Unknown*

For marriage to be a success, every woman and every man should have her and his own bathroom. The end.

– Catherine Zeta-Jones

More marriages might survive if the partners realized that sometimes the better comes after the worse.

– Doug Larson

Remember that creating a successful marriage is like farming: you have to start over again every morning.

– H. Jackson Brown, Jr.

A good marriage is one which allows for change and growth in the individuals and in the way they express their love.

— *Pearl S. Buck*

The greatest marriages are built on teamwork. A mutual respect, a healthy dose of admiration, and a never-ending portion of love and grace.

— *Fawn Weaver*

In good marriages, partners help bandage each other's wounds. More often, we seemed to squeeze lemons over ours.

— *Adam McHugh*

A good marriage, like any partnership, meant subordinating one's own needs to that of the other's, in the expectation that the other will do the same.

— *Nicholas Sparks, True Believer (2003)*

One of the keys to a successful marriage is separate bathrooms. When he enters my bathroom sometimes I'm like, "Why are you in here?" And he's like, "I live here. Can I enjoy my bathroom too?"

— *Michelle Obama*

A good marriage is good because one or both of them have learned to overlook the other's faults, to love the other as they are, and to not attempt to change them or bring them to repentance.

– *Debi Pearl*

Great marriage is not all about a smooth ride, but how you both handle the turbulences.

– *Dr. Lucas D. Shallua*

A successful marriage is based on shared beliefs and respect, not idealistic passions.

– *Lisa Medved, The Engraver's Secret (2024)*

A good marriage is a contest of generosity.

– *Diane Sawyer*

No marriage is perfect. There were times when she gave up on us. There were even more times when I gave up on us. The secret to our longevity is that we never gave up at the same time.

– *Colleen Hoover, All Your Perfects (2018)*

Any good marriage is secret territory, a necessary white space on society's map. What others don't know about it is what makes it yours.

– *Stephen King*

The most important thing for a good marriage is to learn how to argue peaceably.

– *Anita Ekberg*

There is no more lovely, friendly, and charming relationship, communion, or company than a good marriage.

– *Martin Luther*

A good marriage would be between a blind wife and a deaf husband.

– *Michel de Montaigne*

They say that marriage is like a promise, and it is that. But the best ones are based on certainty. An inexplicable faith in someone else.

– *Scottish Queen Mary Stuart*

Fresh-baked cookies do not make a successful marriage… It's knowing each other, valuing the same things, being what the other person can't be, making each other better people.

– *Susan May Warren, You're the One that I Want (2016)*

When a marriage works, nothing on Earth can take its place.

– *U.S. Representative Helen Gahagan Douglas*

CHAPTER 10

Anniversaries

> **A wedding anniversary is the celebration of love, trust, partnership, tolerance, and tenacity. The order varies for any given year.**
> *– Paul Sweeney*

Wedding Anniversary: A yearly event held in a life-long institution where the goal is not to graduate, but to avoid being expelled.

– Craig D. Lounsbrough

Love grows more tremendously full, swift, poignant, as the years multiply.

– Zane Grey

The Cheesecake Factory is a great business model, but if you take your wife there for your 25th wedding anniversary, you might not reach your 26th.

– Scott Adams

An anniversary is a celebration of the triumph and tragedy of love.

– *Debasish Mridha*

Love is not about how many days, months, or years you have been together. Love is about how much you love each other every single day.

– *Unknown*

An anniversary is where you look back at having either fulfilled Cinderella or Lord of the Flies.

– *Fernando A. Torres*

Unless you want to forget your marriage, it's a good idea to remember your anniversary.

– *Melanie White*

We are not the same persons this year as last; nor are those we love. It is a happy chance if we, changing, continue to love a changed person.

– *W. Somerset Maugham*

An anniversary is a time to celebrate the joys of today, the memories of yesterday, and the hopes of tomorrow.

– *Unknown*

Our wedding was many years ago. The celebration continues to this day.

— *Gene Perret*

An anniversary is a reminder as to why you love and married this person.

— *Zoe Foster Blake*

CHAPTER 11

Never!

> **One should always be in love. That's the reason one should never marry.**
> – *Oscar Wilde*

Men are my hobby, if I ever got married I'd have to give it up.

– *Mae West*

Only the deepest love will persuade me into matrimony, which is why I will end up an old maid.

– *Jane Austen, Pride and Prejudice (1813)*

I have come to the conclusion never again to think of marrying, and for this reason, I can never be satisfied with anyone who would be blockhead enough to have me.

– *President Abraham Lincoln*

I disapprove of matrimony as a matter of principle… Why should any independent, intelligent female choose to subject herself to the whims and tyrannies of a husband? I assure you, I have yet to meet a man as sensible as myself!

– *Elizabeth Peters, Crocodile on the Sandbank (1975)*

They ought to find out how to vaccinate for love, like smallpox.

– *Leo Tolstoy, Anna Karenina (1878)*

I'm much happier on my own. I can spend as much time with somebody as I want to spend, but I'm not looking to be with somebody forever or live with someone. I don't want somebody in my house.

– *Whoopi Goldberg*

It is easier to walk these roads alone than it is to drag someone along.

– *Karishma Magvani*

Let me add quickly that I like women, but am a bachelor by choice. While bachelors are lonely people, I'm convinced that married men are lonely people with dependents.

– *Kurt Vonnegut Jr., Look at the Birdie: Unpublished Short Fiction (2009)*

Never marry a man you wouldn't want to be divorced from.

– *Nora Ephron*

Women are like bottles of liquor. They should be sampled, savored, then discarded. Matrimony is for men who can't handle their liquor.

– *Gena Showalter, Deep Kiss of Winter (2009)*

Never get married in college; it's hard to get a start if a prospective employer finds you've already made one mistake.

– *Elbert Hubbard*

I'd rather be single, happy, and lonely sometimes than married, lonely, and happy sometimes.

– *Mark Fiore, You Are Loved… An Email Memoir (2012)*

Never marry a person that feels superior to you.

– *Fela Bank-Olemoh*

It would take a hell of a wife to beat no wife at all.

– *Cormac McCarthy, The Crossing (1994)*

Man marries himself if he never wants to be married.

– *Tamerlan Kuzgov*

A marriage of two independent and equally irritable intelligences seems to me reckless to the point of insanity.

– Dorothy L. Sayers, *Gaudy Night* (1935)

Why should love require a contract? Why put yourself into the clutches of the state and give it power over you? Why invite lawyers to f*ck around with your assets? Marriage is for the immature and the insecure and the ignorant. We who see through such institutions should be content to live together without legal coercion.

– Robert Silverberg

Oh, Lizzy! Do anything rather than marry without affection.

– Jane Austen, *Pride and Prejudice* (1813)

Why is it that married people always say "Come in" when everything they do says "Get out"? They talk about their miseries and then ask you why you're unmarried.

– Malcolm Bradbury, *The History Man* (1975)

One can be very much in love with a woman without wishing to spend the rest of one's life with her.

– W. Somerset Maugham, *The Painted Veil* (1925)

Perhaps I won't marry then. Instead, you and I shall live as spinsters in a cottage by the sea. We'll burn our corsets, eat chocolate morning, noon and night and grow fat as hedgehogs.

– *Alyxandra Harvey,* Haunting Violet *(2011)*

I am your Prince and you will marry me," Humperdinck said.
Buttercup whispered, "I am your servant and I refuse."
"I am your Prince and you cannot refuse."
"I am your loyal servant and I just did."
"Refusal means death."
"Kill me then."

– *William Goldman,* The Princess Bride *(1973)*

I don't want to be married just to be married. I can't think of anything lonelier than spending the rest of my life with someone I can't talk to, or worse, someone I can't be silent with.

– *Mary Ann Shaffer,* The Guernsey Literary and Potato Peel Pie Society *(2008)*

I know enough to know that no woman should ever marry a man who hated his mother.

– *Martha Gellhorn,* Selected Letters *(2006)*

If I have to "catch" a man to get a husband, I don't want one.

– *Tamora Pierce,* Shatterglass *(2003)*

Never marry at all, Dorian. Men marry because they are tired, women, because they are curious: both are disappointed.

– *Oscar Wilde, The Picture of Dorian Gray (1890)*

Better die an old maid, sister, than marry the wrong man.

– *Billy Sunday*

To marry is to narrow one's possibilities horribly.

– *Jude Morgan, Indiscretion (2005)*

There are some who want to get married and others who don't. I have never had an impulse to go to the altar. I am a difficult person to lead.

– *Greta Garbo, Greta & Cecil (1994)*

"I'm not married," he said softly, "because I can't stomach the idea of marrying a woman inferior to me in mind and spirit. It would mean the death of my soul."

– *Sarah J. Maas, Throne of Glass (2012)*

For better, for worse?
F*ck. That. Sh*t.

– *Colleen Hoover, It Ends with Us (2016)*

CHAPTER 12

Divorce

> **My husband and I have never considered divorce...
> murder sometimes, but never divorce.**
> – *Joyce Brothers*

Hollywood brides keep the bouquets and throw away the grooms.

– *Groucho Marx*

Getting divorced just because you don't love a man is almost as silly as getting married just because you do.

– *Zsa Zsa Gabor*

There are things in my life that are hard to reconcile, like divorce. Sometimes it is very difficult to make sense of how it could possibly happen. Laying blame is so easy. I don't have time for hate or negativity in my life. There's no room for it.

– *Reese Witherspoon*

You can always tell how successful a man is when his divorced wife still bears his name.

– *Nkwachukwu Ogbuagu*

Half of all marriages end in divorce – and then there are the really unhappy ones.

– *Joan Rivers*

Women leave their marriages when they can't take any more. Men leave when they find someone new.

– *J. Courtney Sullivan, Commencement (2009)*

"Well, we've never had a divorce in our family," Aurora said, "but if we have to have one, Tomas is a good place to start."

– *Larry McMurtry, Terms of Endearment (1975)*

Those who get married for the wrong reasons often get divorced for the right ones.

– *Omar Cherif*

Heartbreak is a loss. Divorce is a piece of paper.

– *Taylor Jenkins Reid, The Seven Husbands of Evelyn Hugo (2017)*

It is even more painful to have your heart broken by someone who you know does not deserve you.

— *Mokokoma Mokhonoana*

Some people are addicted to wedding cakes and divorces.

— *Steven Magee*

Divorce is a process, not an event. It takes months to unfold, a barrage of emotional ups and downs as denial is replaced by grief, grief by anger, and anger gradually eases into acceptance.

— *M.K. Tod, Time and Regret (2016)*

You didn't grow apart because you're evil, but because you evolved. It's life. It's natural. It's ok. Keep growing!

— *Curtis Tyrone Jones*

You ended one life, but I got another in me.

— *L.M. Browning, Drive Through the Night (2022)*

Divorce is overcome by overlooking offense.

— *Khuliso Mamathoni, The Greatest Proposal (2016)*

Losing a mate to death is devastating but it's not a personal attack like divorce. When somebody you love stops loving you and walks away, it's an insult beyond comparison.

– *Sue Merrell, Great News Town (2011)*

The failure of marriage reveals your failures.

– *Tamerlan Kuzgov*

People do not get married planning to divorce. Divorce is the result of a lack of preparation for marriage and the failure to learn the skills of working together as teammates in an intimate relationship.

– *Gary Chapman, Things I Wish I'd Known Before We Got Married (2010)*

Divorce is success. Failure is staying married to a person you no longer love.

– *Ben Tolosa, Masterplan Your Success: Deadline Your Dreams (2017)*

If you really want to get to know someone, you have to divorce him.

– *Elizabeth Gilbert, Eat, Pray, Love (2006)*

The man who leaves you is simply clearing the way for the one you deserve.

– *Naide P. Obiang*

Divorce = Rebirth: forget the past, replan your life, improve your appearance & REJUVENATE!

– *Rossana Condoleo*

The reason why people in traditional marriages tend to stay together for a lifetime is because it is "standard" to sacrifice novelty for longevity, while some of us [the modern ones] who value sensuality and depth of connection in a relationship or marriage find it absolutely preposterous to sacrifice novelty for longevity – the price is just way too high, that is if you truly understand what's really at stake.

– *Lebo Grand*

When you divorce someone, you divorce their whole family, Madeline had told her once.

– *Liane Moriarty, Big Little Lies (2014)*

Immediately after a divorce or a breakup, your mind whispers that there are plenty more fish in the sea, while your heart shouts that there is only one whoever-you-just-divorced-or-broke-up-with.

– *Mokokoma Mokhonoana*

Divorce is a fire exit. When a house is burning, it doesn't matter who set the fire. If there is no fire exit, everyone in the house will be burned!

— *Mehmet Murat ildan*

If I follow the inclination of my nature, it is this: beggar-woman and single, far rather than queen and married.

— *Elizabeth I, Collected Works (2000)*

The hard truth of the dissolution of a marriage is that, while it takes two to say "I do," it takes only one to say "I don't."

— *Nicole Sodoma, Please Don't Say You're Sorry: An Empowering Perspective on Marriage, Separation, and Divorce from a Marriage-Loving Divorce Attorney (2022)*

Sometimes divorce isn't an earth-shattering loss. Sometimes it's just two people waking up out of a fog.

— *Taylor Jenkins Reid, The Seven Husbands of Evelyn Hugo (2017)*

At the end of a marriage, no one wins. There is only anger, sorrow, guilt, emptiness, and defeat.

— *Padma Lakshmi, Love, Loss, and What We Ate: A Memoir (2013)*

Some people rushed into divorce even faster than they rushed into marriage.

— *Mokokoma Mokhonoana*

When a woman thinks her husband is a fool, her marriage is over. They may part in one year or ten; they may live together until death. But if she thinks he is a fool, she will not love him again.

— *Philippa Gregory, The Other Queen (2008)*

Divorce takes the cross off the parent's shoulders, and places it on their children's.

— *Allene van Oirschot, Daddy's Little Girl (2010)*

Divorce isn't the child's fault. Don't say anything unkind about your ex to the child because you're really just hurting the child.

— *Valerie Bertinelli*

Once that ship has sailed, don't hold on to the anchor.

— *Stanley Victor Paskavich*

You can get married in an hour, but it typically takes a year to get divorced.

— *Steven Magee*

Adrian Mole's father was so angry that so many people got divorced nowadays. HE had been unhappily married for 30 years, why should everybody else get away?

— *Sue Townsend*

The snag about marriage is it isn't worth the divorce.

— *Suzanne Finnamore, Split: A Memoir of Divorce (2008)*

Divorce isn't such a tragedy. A tragedy's staying in an unhappy marriage, teaching your children the wrong things about love. Nobody ever died of divorce.

— *Jennifer Weiner, Fly Away Home (2010)*

Divorce is an expensive punishment love gets when it fails.

— *Bangambiki Habyarimana, The Great Pearl of Wisdom (2015)*

They throw rice at a new marriage, then give him beans in a divorce.

— *Anthony Liccione*

Love is so powerful that some people pretend to be smart, someone they are not, kind, reasonable, and/or interested in things they really hate… for a very long time, until the relationship or marriage ends, or seems to be about to end.

— *Mokokoma Mokhonoana*

It's hard to admit that a marriage might be over when the love is still there. People are led to believe that a marriage ends only when the love has been lost; when anger replaces happiness when contempt replaces bliss. But Graham and I aren't angry with each other, we're just not the same people we used to be.

– *Colleen Hoover*

When mom and dad went to war, the only prisoners they took were the children.

– *Pat Conroy*

In every marriage more than a week old there are grounds for divorce. The trick is to find and continue to find grounds for marriage.

– *Robert Anderson*

I always feel that a man and a woman, who do not like the same films, will eventually divorce.

– *Jean-Luc Godard*

The obvious effect of frivolous divorce will be frivolous marriage. If people can be separated for no reason they will feel it all the easier to be united for no reason.

– *G.K. Chesterton, The Superstition of Divorce (2003)*

If you have to convince someone to stay with you then they have already left.

– *Shannon L. Alder*

They ought to do away with divorce settlements. Instead, both parties should flip a coin. The winner gets to stay where he or she is and keep everything. The loser goes to Paraguay. That's it.

– *Suzanne Finnamore, Split: A Memoir of Divorce (2008)*

Trust me, divorce is not a hall pass. While it can feel like freedom to some, it can feel like death to others. Either way, it inevitably comes rushing upstream carrying a containership of grief and guilt. It's like a bad dream, even when you didn't realize you were asleep.

– *Nicole Sodoma, Please Don't Say You're Sorry: An Empowering Perspective on Marriage, Separation, and Divorce from a Marriage-Loving Divorce Attorney (2022)*

Bad divorce?" Hardy asked, his gaze falling to my hands. I realized I was clutching my purse in a death grip. "No, the divorce was great," I said. "It was the marriage that sucked."

– *Lisa Kleypas, Blue-Eyed Devil (2008)*

Oftentimes someone leaves their partner who is comparable to the sun for someone else who is comparable to a spark.

– *Mokokoma Mokhonoana*

There is no loneliness like that of a failed marriage.

— *Alexander Theroux*

Do not let your divorce define you and the rest of your life. Let go of anger and embrace the future possibilities of infinitesimal happiness.

— *Divorce Goddess*

The end is almost always the beginning of something better.

— *Kevin Kelly, Excellent Advice for Living: Wisdom I Wish I'd Known Earlier (2023)*

CHAPTER 13

Religious Teachings

> **Marriage may be the closest thing to Heaven
> or Hell any of us will know on this earth.**
> *– Edwin Louis Cole*

Marriage is not just spiritual communion; it is also remembering to take out the trash.

— *Joyce Brothers*

The Lord God said, "It is not good for the man to be alone. I will make a helper suitable for him."

— *Genesis 2:18, Holy Bible (New International Version)*

An ideal marriage is a true partnership between two imperfect people, each striving to complement the other, to keep the Commandments, and to do the will of the Lord.

— *LDS Church President Russell M. Nelson*

He who finds a wife finds what is good and receives favor from the Lord.

— *Proverbs 18:22, Holy Bible (New International Version)*

Marriage is an act of will that signifies and involves a mutual gift, which unites the spouses and binds them to their eventual souls, with whom they make up a sole family - a domestic church.

— *Pope John Paul II*

"Haven't you read," he replied, "that at the beginning the Creator 'made them male and female,' and said, 'For this reason a man will leave his father and mother and be united to his wife, and the two will become one flesh'? So they are no longer two, but one flesh. Therefore what God has joined together, let no one separate."

— *Matthew 19:4-6, Holy Bible (New International Version)*

They say all marriages are made in heaven, but so are thunder and lightning.

— *Clint Eastwood*

Be devoted to one another in love. Honor one another above yourselves.

— *Romans 12:10, Holy Bible (New International Version)*

God gets glory when two very different and very imperfect people forge a life of faithfulness in the furnace of affliction by relying on Christ.

– *John Piper*

Houses and wealth are inherited from parents, but a prudent wife is from the Lord.

– *Proverbs 19:14, Holy Bible (New International Version)*

Living together is an art. It's a patient art, it's a beautiful art, it's fascinating.

– *Pope Francis*

Let marriage be held in honor among all, and let the marriage bed be undefiled, for God will judge the sexually immoral and adulterous.

– *Hebrews 13:4, Holy Bible (New International Version)*

Marriage is a very sacred institution and should not be degraded by allowing every other type of relationship to be made equivalent to it.

– *U.S. Secretary of Housing and Urban Development Ben Carson*

Better to live on a corner of the roof than in a house shared with a quarrelsome wife.

– *Proverbs 21:9, Holy Bible (New International Version)*

If God had a wife, He would be in just as much trouble as any man.

– *Matshona Dhliwayo*

Husbands, in the same way be considerate as you live with your wives, and treat them with respect as the weaker partner and as heirs with you of the gracious gift of life, so that nothing will hinder your prayers.

– *1 Peter 3:7, Holy Bible (New International Version)*

Every major religion on earth subscribes to the belief in a period of fasting – abstinence from food, sex, and other basic human cravings. It's meant to help you dwell on the bigger mysteries that have confounded mankind – the purpose of existence, the meaning of life, the transient effervescence of our being and… what your wife really meant when she said, "I am not mad at you" this morning.

– *Tarika Roy and Soumya Gupta, Mad(e) In India (2021)*

Do not be yoked together with unbelievers. For what do righteousness and wickedness have in common? Or what fellowship can light have with darkness?

– *2 Corinthians 6:14, Holy Bible (New International Version)*

She is the crescendo, the final, astonishing work of God. Woman. In one last flourish, creation comes to a finish with Eve. She is the Master's finishing touch.

– *John Elderedge*

Wives, submit to your husbands, as is fitting in the Lord. Husbands, love your wives, and do not be harsh with them.

– *Colossians 3:18-19, Holy Bible (New International Version)*

Eve was not taken out of Adam's head to top him, neither out of his feet to be trampled on by him, but out of his side to be equal with him, under his arm to be protected by him, and near his heart to be loved by him.

– *Matthew Henry*

A wife of noble character who can find? She is worth far more than rubies.

– *Proverbs 31:10, Holy Bible (New International Version)*

God proved two things when He brought us together: His genius and His sense of humor.

– *Unknown*

No human law can abolish the natural and original right of marriage, nor in any way limit the chief and principal purpose of marriage ordained by God's authority from the beginning: "Increase and multiply."

– *Pope Leo XIII*

Wives, submit yourselves to your own husbands as you do to the Lord. For the husband is the head of the wife as Christ is the head of the church, his body, of which he is the Savior. Now as the church submits to Christ, so also wives should submit to their husbands in everything.

Husbands, love your wives, just as Christ loved the church and gave himself up for her to make her holy, cleansing her by the washing with water through the word, and to present her to himself as a radiant church, without stain or wrinkle or any other blemish, but holy and blameless. In this same way, husbands ought to love their wives as their own bodies. He who loves his wife loves himself. After all, no one ever hated their own body, but they feed and care for their body, just as Christ does the church – for we are members of his body. "For this reason a man will leave his father and mother and be united to his wife, and the two will become one flesh." This is a profound mystery – but I am talking about Christ and the church. However, each one of you also must love his wife as he loves himself, and the wife must respect her husband.

– *Ephesians 5:22-33, Holy Bible (New International Version)*

But since sexual immorality is occurring, each man should have sexual relations with his own wife, and each woman with her own husband. The husband should fulfill his marital duty to his wife, and likewise the wife to her husband. The wife does not have authority over her own body but yields it to her husband. In the same way, the husband does not have authority over his own body but yields it to his wife. Do not deprive each other except perhaps by mutual consent and for a time, so that you may devote yourselves to prayer. Then come together again so that Satan will not tempt you because of your lack of self-control. I say this as a concession, not as a command. I wish that all of you were as I am. But each of you has your own gift from God; one has this gift, another has that.

Now to the unmarried and the widows I say: It is good for them to stay unmarried, as I do. But if they cannot control themselves, they should marry, for it is better to marry than to burn with passion.

To the married I give this command (not I, but the Lord): A wife must not separate from her husband. But if she does, she must remain unmarried or else be reconciled to her husband. And a husband must not divorce his wife.

– *1 Corinthians 7:2-11, Holy Bible (New International Version)*

God is the author of the marriage, but we are the engineers who design and steer it in the direction that we wish.

– *Dr. Lucas D. Shallua*

Be devoted to one another in love. Honor one another above yourselves.

– *Romans 12:10, Holy Bible (New International Version)*

I tell you that anyone who divorces his wife, except for sexual immorality, and marries another woman commits adultery.

– *Matthew 19:9, Holy Bible (New International Version)*

Just as a father hates cancer, because of what it does to his child, so God hates divorce, because of what it does to His children.

– *Kyle Idleman, AHA: The God Moment That Changes Everything (2014)*

If a man has recently married, he must not be sent to war or have any other duty laid on him. For one year he is to be free to stay at home and bring happiness to the wife he has married.

– *Deuteronomy 24:5, Holy Bible (New International Version)*

Marriages are made in heaven. When Allah made a creature, He also made the creature's mate.

– *Farahad Zama, The Wedding Wallah (2011)*

Love is patient, love is kind. It does not envy, it does not boast, it is not proud. It does not dishonor others, it is not self-seeking, it is not easily angered, it keeps no record of wrongs.

– *1 Corinthians 13:4-5, Holy Bible (New International Version)*

If Catholics would simply live the Sacrament of Matrimony for one generation, we would witness a transformation of society and have a Christian culture.

– *Scott Hahn, The First Society: The Sacrament of Matrimony and the Restoration of the Social Order (2018)*

As a young man marries a young woman, so will your Builder marry you; as a bridegroom rejoices over his bride, so will your God rejoice over you.

– *Isaiah 62:5, Holy Bible (New International Version)*

Real love, the Bible says, instinctively desires permanence.

– Timothy Keller, *The Meaning of Marriage: Facing the Complexities of Commitment with the Wisdom of God (2011)*

A wife of noble character is her husband's crown, but a disgraceful wife is like decay in his bones.

– *Proverbs 12:4, Holy Bible (New International Version)*

God gave marriage as a living illustration of the relationship between Christ and his church (Ephesians 5:32). If you want to teach the world the love of God, become husband who loves his wife as Christ loves the church (Ephesians 5:25). If you want to teach the world how the church submits to the Lord, become a wife who submits to her husband (Ephesians 5:22-24).

– Voddie T. Baucham Jr., *What He Must Be …If He Wants to Marry My Daughter (2009)*

"There are three things that are too amazing for me, four that I do not understand: the way of an eagle in the sky, the way of a snake on a rock, the way of a ship on the high seas, and the way of a man with a young woman.

– *Proverbs 30:18-19, Holy Bible (New International Version)*

You are altogether beautiful, my darling; there is no flaw in you.

– *Song of Songs 4:7*

Two practicing Christians can never divorce.

– *Fela Bank-Olemoh*

Catholics don't believe in divorce. We do believe in murder. There's always Confession, after all.

– *Diana Gabaldon, An Echo in the Bone (2009)*

Love is moral even without legal marriage, but marriage is immoral without love.

– *Ellen Key*

You are never more like Jesus than when you are loving someone who is not loving you in return. That is gospel love.

– *Brandon Michael West, It Is Not Your Business to Succeed: Your Role in Leadership When You Can't Control Your Outcomes (2024)*

Natural marriage, therefore, is fully understood in the light of its fulfilment in the sacrament of Matrimony: only in contemplating Christ does a person come to know the deepest truth about human relationships.

– *Pope Francis*

We must say to ourselves something like this: Well, when Jesus looked down from the cross, he didn't think, I am giving myself to you because you are so attractive to me. No, he was in agony, and he looked down at us – denying him, abandoning him, and betraying him – and in the greatest act of love in history, he STAYED. He said, Father, forgive them, they don't know what they are doing. He loved us, not because we were lovely to him, but to make us lovely. That is why I am going to love my spouse. Speak to your heart like that, and then fulfill the promises you made on your wedding day.

– Timothy Keller, *The Meaning of Marriage: Facing the Complexities of Commitment with the Wisdom of God (2011)*

In marriage, romance is meant to thrive and vibrantly flourish. Both the Old and New Testaments commend the beauty of sexual love within the context of matrimony.

– Alex Kendrick, *The Love Dare (2008)*

No woman wants to be in submission to a man who isn't in submission to God!

– T.D. Jakes

Whatever Jesus lays His hands upon, lives. If He lays His hands upon a marriage, it lives. If He is allowed to lay His hands on the family, it lives.

– LDS Church President Howard W. Hunter

To the young couples, go build your marriage and family the way you want, but always make your creator the central pillar of the structure you establish.

– Dr. Lucas D. Shallua

To be loved but not known is comforting, but superficial. To be known and not loved is our greatest fear. But to be fully known and truly loved is, well, a lot like being loved by God. It is what we need more than anything. It liberates us from pretense, humbles us out of our self-righteousness, and fortifies us for any difficulty life can throw at us.

– Timothy Keller, *The Meaning of Marriage: Facing the Complexities of Commitment with the Wisdom of God* (2011)

When you are still dating, the devil is on your side, he is a fan of dating. However, the day you decide to get married officially, and the blessing of God is pronounced upon your life, the devil becomes your great enemy and destroyer of your marriage.

– Khuliso Mamathoni, *The Greatest Proposal* (2016)

It takes three to make love, not two: you, your spouse, and God. Without God people only succeed in bringing out the worst in one another. Lovers who have nothing else to do but love each other soon find there is nothing else. Without a central loyalty life is unfinished.

– Fulton J. Sheen, *Seven Words of Jesus and Mary: Lessons from Cana and Calvary* (1945)

The remedy for most marital stress is not in divorce. It is in repentance and forgiveness, in sincere expressions of charity and service. It is not in separation. It is in simple integrity that leads a man and a woman to square up their shoulders and meet their obligations. It is found in the Golden Rule, a time-honored principle that should first and foremost find expression in marriage.

– Gordon B. Hinckley, *Standing for Something: 10 Neglected Virtues That Will Heal Our Hearts and Homes* (2000)

Husbands and wives, recognize that in marriage you have become one flesh. If you live for your private pleasure at the expense of your spouse, you are living against yourself and destroying your joy. But if you devote yourself with all your heart to the holy joy of your spouse, you will also be living for your joy and making a marriage after the image of Christ and His church.

– John Piper

If a man and a woman marry in order to be companions on the journey from earth to heaven, then their union will bring great joy to themselves and to others.

– John Chrysostom, *On Living Simply: The Golden Voice of John Chrysostom* (1997)

CHAPTER 14

Happily Ever After

> **My wife and I were happy for twenty years. Then we met.**
> *– Rodney Dangerfield*

We are happily married. She is happily, and I am married.

– *Anoir Ou-Chad*

In a happy marriage it is the wife who provides the climate, the husband the landscape.

– *Gerald Brenan*

The secret of a happy marriage remains a secret.

– *Henny Youngman*

Love one another and you will be happy. It's as simple and as difficult as that.

— *Michael Leunig*

You can measure the happiness of a marriage by the number of scars that each partner carries on their tongues, earned from years of biting back angry words.

— *Elizabeth Gilbert, Committed: A Skeptic Makes Peace with Marriage (2009)*

Happy marriages begin when we marry the ones we love, and they blossom when we love the ones we marry.

— *Tom Mullen*

When you end up happily married, even the failed relationships have worked beautifully to get you there.

— *Julia Roberts*

The secret to a happy marriage is if you can be at peace with someone within four walls, if you are content because the one you love is near to you, either upstairs or downstairs, or in the same room, and you feel that warmth that you don't find very often, then that is what love is all about.

— *Bruce Forsyth*

A happy marriage is a long conversation which always seems too short.

— *Andre Marois*

The cynic will tell you that married happiness is a matter of give and take. Do not believe him; it is a matter of give and give.

— *Ronald Knox, Bridegroom and Bride (1957)*

The secret of a happy marriage is finding the right person. You know they're right if you love to be with them all the time.

— *Julia Child*

A happy marriage is the union of two good forgivers.

— *Ruth Bell Graham*

Be careful whom you choose to love. This decision will impact your future life and happiness in ways you cannot yet imagine.

— *Toni Coleman*

There is no greater happiness for a man than approaching a door at the end of a day knowing someone on the other side of that door is waiting for the sound of his footsteps.

— *President Ronald Reagan*

I have learned that only two things are necessary to keep one's wife happy. First, let her think she's having her own way. And second, let her have it.

— *President Lyndon B. Johnson*

We Greeks get married in circles, to impress upon ourselves the essential matrimonial facts: that to be happy you have to find variety in repetition; that to go forward you have to come back to where you begin.

— *Jeffrey Eugenides, Middlesex (2002)*

And not telling anyone anything whenever possible is the secret of a happy marriage, in my experience.

— *Penny Vincenzi, No Angel (2000)*

You want to know the secret to raising good kids?

What's that? asked Thomas.

High expectations.

Thomas laughed. Alright, well what's the secret to a happy marriage?

Clyde smiled back, but his face started to fall, and he chose his words carefully. Low expectations.

— *Chris Nicolaisen, The Life and Death of the Ericsons (2013)*

You'll be happy if you'll remember that men don't change much. Women do. Women adapt themselves, and if you think that means they lose their individuality, you're wrong. Show me a happy marriage and I'll show you a clever woman.

– Elizabeth Cadell

The sooner men learn to make companions and equals of their wives and not subordinates, the sooner the marriage relation will be one of harmony.

– Lucy Parsons

Sensual pleasures have the fleeting brilliance of a comet; a happy marriage has the tranquility of a lovely sunset.

– Ann Landers

Happiness in marriage is entirely a matter of chance.

– Jane Austen

What counts in making a happy marriage is not so much how compatible you are, but how you deal with incompatibility.

– Leo Tolstoy

Some people ask the secret of our long marriage. We take time to go to a restaurant two times a week. A little candlelight, dinner, soft music, and dancing. She goes Tuesdays, I go Fridays.

– *Henny Youngman*

The highest happiness on earth is marriage.

– *William Lyon Phelps*

CHAPTER 15

Miscellaneous

> **To marry is to halve your rights and double your duties.**
> – *Arthur Schopenhauer*

Matrimony and firefighting. They ain't for cowards.

– *Lois Greiman, Unplugged (2006)*

To get the full value of joy you must have someone to divide it with.

– *Mark Twain*

Women marry thinking their chosen men would change, and they don't! Men marry thinking their chosen counterpart won't change, and they do!!

– *Sandeep Sahajpal, The Twelfth Preamble: To all the authors to be! (2017)*

The value of marriage is not that adults produce children, but that children produce adults.

— *Peter De Vries*

Is anybody really ready to get married? I doubt it. Nobody's ready for marriage. Marriage makes you ready for marriage!

— *Schnarch David, Passionate Marriage (1997)*

I know not which lives more unnatural lives, obeying husbands, or commanding wives.

— *U.S. Founding Father Benjamin Franklin*

A man marries a woman when she feels like home.

— *Tiffany Majors*

Marriage without struggle is like an unfired clay pot. It is easily made, but it will not stand the test of time.

— *Allan Wolf, The Watch That Ends the Night (2011)*

What we do for each other before marriage is no indication of what we will do after marriage.

— *Gary Chapman, The Five Love Languages: How to Express Heartfelt Commitment to Your Mate (1990)*

Who won in life? Me. Because I got to marry you.

– *Chip Gaines*

More beautiful than marrying the man you love, Rozalka, is the joy of loving the man you married.

– *Sarah Brazytis, The Reluctant Bride (2019)*

There are guys who grow up thinking they'll settle down some distant time in the future, and there are guys who are ready for marriage as soon as they meet the right person. The former bore me, mainly because they're pathetic; and the latter, frankly are hard to find.

– *Nicholas Sparks, The Last Song (2009)*

Why does a woman work ten years to change a man, then complain he's not the man she married?

– *Barbra Streisand*

Maybe you expected marriage to be perfect – I guess that's where you and I are different. See, I thought it would be all about making mistakes, but doing it with someone who's there to remind you what you learned along the way.

– *Jodi Picoult, Handle with Care (2009)*

She believed in love, but not matrimony; she believed in education, but not degrees.

— *Harrshada Deshpande, Megh: A Heartwarming Love Story of a Genius (2023)*

Sexiness wears thin after awhile and beauty fades, but to be married to a man who makes you laugh every day, ah, now that is a treat.

— *Joanne Woodward*

My wife has lived with at least five different men since we were wed – and each of the five has been me.

— *Timothy J. Keller, The Meaning of Marriage: Facing the Complexities of Commitment with the Wisdom of God (2011)*

Think of your husband as a house. You are allowed to give him a fresh coat of paint and change out the furniture now and then. But if you're constantly trying to pour a new foundation or replace the roof, you're in serious trouble.

— *Peter Scott, There's a Spouse in My House: A Humorous Journey Through the First Years of Marriage (2008)*

Some marriages are made in heaven, but they all have to be maintained on earth.

— *Debbie Macomber, Mrs. Miracle (1996)*

Married people use a successful marriage as an advertisement for marriage, and a failed marriage as an advertisement for a good husband or wife.

— *Mokokoma Mokhonoana*

A marriage doesn't mean that the husband will be married to his wife.

— *Tamerlan Kuzgov*

Some people want or wanted to be married as soon as possible, so they can or could finally stop pretending to be worth marrying.

— *Mokokoma Mokhonoana*

There should be Oscars for real life, and we should give them to all the people who are still married.

— *Hannah Moskowitz, Sick Kids in Love (2019)*

People stand in front of an officiant and say "I do," but that shouldn't mean "I'm done" when it comes to putting time and effort to grow their relationship.

— *Beth Ehemann, Room for More (2014)*

Marriage isn't for the weak or lazy. It's work, and it should be. What would be the point otherwise?

— *J.D. Robb, Portrait in Death (2003)*

Love is an ideal thing, marriage a real thing.

— *Johann Wolfgang von Goethe*

We have a couple of rules in our relationship. The first rule is that I make her feel like she's getting everything. The second rule is that I actually do let her have her way in everything. And, so far, it's working.

— *Justin Timberlake*

In their hearts, women think that it is the men's business to earn money and theirs to spend it – if possible during their husband's life, but, at any rate, after his death.

— *Arthur Schopenhauer, On Women (1851)*

To marry for support is legal prostitution.

— *Mary Wollstonecraft, A Vindication of the Rights of Woman (2022)*

Some women marry houses.

— *Anne Sexton*

You should get married only when you got the ability to survive the world alone.

— *P.S. Jagadeesh Kumar*

Either you go to America with Mrs. Van Hopper or you come home to Manderley with me.

Do you mean you want a secretary or something?

No, I'm asking you to marry me, you little fool.

– *Daphne du Maurier, Rebecca (1938)*

Marriage usually ends up turning one of the spouses into the other.

– *Mokokoma Mokhonoana*

To catch a husband is an art; to hold him is a job.

– *Simone de Beauvoir, The Second Sex (1949)*

Someday, you may think of marrying. Pick someone who thinks you're the only person in the room.

– *Gabrielle Zevin, The Storied Life of A.J. Fikry (2014)*

Well married, a man is winged – ill-matched, he is shackled.

– *Henry Ward Beecher, Norwood: or, Village life in New England (1867)*

Here's my advice to you: don't marry until you can tell yourself that you've done all you could, and until you've stopped loving the women you've chosen, until you see her clearly, otherwise you'll be cruelly and irremediably mistaken. Marry when you're old and good for nothing… Otherwise, all that's good and lofty in you will be lost.

– *Leo Tolstoy, War and Peace (1868)*

In marriage, each partner is to be an encourager rather than a critic; a forgiver rather than a collector of hurts; an enabler rather than a reformer.

– *H. Norman Wright*

"I've learned this much about marriage," he said now. "You get tested. You find out who you are, who the other person is, and how you accommodate or don't."

– *Mitch Albom, Tuesdays with Morrie (1997)*

A man should be taller, older, heavier, uglier, and hoarser than his wife.

– *E.W. Howe*

Nobles and peasants marry early. Businessmen tend to wait.

– *David Eddings, Polgara the Sorceress (1997)*

But if as you read this book you're saying to yourself: "I'd rather be miserably married than be alone." Well young lady, take out your clown shoes and buckle your seat belt – it's going to be a very bumpy, one-woman circus.

– *Osayi Osar-Emokpae, Impossible Is Stupid (2011)*

Think not because you are now wed, that all your courtship's at an end.

– *Antonio Hurtado de Mendoza*

Find a woman who makes you feel more alive. She won't make life perfect, but she'll make it infinitely more interesting. And then love her with all that's in you.

– *Gayle G. Roper, Shadows on the Sand (2011)*

There are often two conversations going on in a marriage. The one that you're having and the one you're not.

– *Robin Black, Life Drawing (2014)*

The rule seemed to be that a great woman must either die unwed… or find a still greater man to marry her. … The great man, on the other hand, could marry where he liked, not being restricted to great women; indeed, it was often found sweet and commendable in him to choose a woman of no sort of greatness at all.

– *Dorothy L. Sayers, Gaudy Night (1935)*

Love at first sight is easy to understand; it's when two people have been looking at each other for a lifetime that it becomes a miracle.

— *Sam Levenson*

Mom, camping is not a date; it's an endurance test. If you can survive camping with someone, you should marry them on the way home.

— *Yvonne Prinz, The Vinyl Princess (2009)*

A woman is not property, and husbands who think otherwise are living in a dreamworld.

— *Robert A. Heinlein, Time Enough for Love (1973)*

You need to play to your strengths as a couple. Sharing is really awesome when you're messing around with Play-Doh in kindergarten. It's less awesome when you're adults and one of you is good at something and the other person sucks at it. So just let the more skilled person take the reins.

— *Peter Scott, There's a Spouse in My House: A Humorous Journey Through the First Years of Marriage (2008)*

If I had a girl I should say to her, "Marry for love if you can. It won't last, but it is a very interesting experience and makes a good beginning in life. Later on, when you marry for money, for heaven's sake let it be big money. There are no other possible reasons for marrying at all."

— *Nancy Mitford, Christmas Pudding (1932)*

No woman marries for money; they are all clever enough, before marrying a millionaire, to fall in love with him first.

– *Cesare Pavese*

What a man wants is a mate and what a woman wants is infinite security, and what a man is is an arrow into the future and a what a woman is is the place the arrow shoots off from.

– *Sylvia Plath, The Bell Jar (1963)*

There is no such thing as a perfect match. There are only somewhat good and somewhat bad matches. A couple are like two pebbles that are next to each other on a beach. They will have rough edges and rub each other the wrong way initially. But as they spend time together and the waves pound them, the edges rub off and they will seem made for each other.

– *Farahad Zama, The Many Conditions of Love (2009)*

You know it's never fifty-fifty in a marriage. It's always seventy-thirty, or sixty-forty. Someone falls in love first. Someone puts someone else up on a pedestal. Someone works very hard to keep things rolling smoothly; someone else sails along for the ride.

– *Jodi Picoult, Mercy (1996)*

Chains do not hold a marriage together. It is threads, hundreds of tiny threads, which sew people together through the years.

– *Simone Signoret*

Marriage must fight constantly against a monster which devours everything: routine.

— *Honore de Balzac*

Something my dad says… He says you end up marrying the one you don't understand. Then you spend the rest of your life trying.

— *Frederik Backman, Anxious People (2019)*

The problem with marriage is that it ends every night after making love, and it must be rebuilt every morning before breakfast.

— *Gabriel García Márquez*

In the true married relationship, the independence of husband and wife will be equal, their dependence mutual, and their obligations reciprocal.

— *Lucretia Mott*

"Whoa, I'm your girlfriend now?"

Archer shrugged. "We've tried to kill each other, fought ghouls, and kissed a lot. I'm pretty sure we're married in some cultures."

— *Rachel Hawkins, Spell Bound (2012)*

CONCLUSION

> The real act of marriage takes place in the heart, not in the ballroom or church or synagogue. It's a choice you make – not just on your wedding day, but over and over again – and that choice is reflected in the way you treat your husband or wife.
> – *Barbara de Angelis*

Photo Courtesy of Little Chapel of Hearts (Las Vegas)

To summarize the above quotes, marriage is:

1. a sacred union between two imperfect individuals who commit their remaining days on earth to each other,

2. a special friendship that offers unwavering support, hope, and encouragement,

3. an endless source of love, happiness, and intimacy (which hopefully outweighs the occasional anger, frustration, and hurt feelings),

4. a blessing from God (so never take your spouse for granted!), and

5. an opportunity to grow and develop as individuals and as a couple.

The differing perspectives and advice given on this important topic are as numerous as the number of folks who get married each year – which explains why it was relatively easy to find the 519 marriage quotes contained in this book.

The bottom line is that the institution of marriage is a precious gift and requires the loving couple to make a binding, life-long commitment to continually work on their relationship. In any case, I hope the quotes above made you laugh and perhaps think a little deeper about this important subject.

But wait, there's more! I saved the best for last. Below is the TOP TEN LIST of my all-time favorite marriage quotes.

10. Marriage is not 50-50. Divorce is 50-50. Marriage has to be 100-100. It isn't dividing everything in half, but giving everything you've got!

– *Dave Willis*

9. A good marriage is where both people feel like they're getting the better end of the deal.

– *Anne Lamott, Joe Jones (1986)*

8. A wedding is an event. A marriage is a lifetime.

– *Alisa DiLorenzo, The 6 Pillars of Intimacy Conflict Resolution: The Secret to Breaking the Conflict Cycle in Your Marriage (2023)*

7. Marriage is not the end of the search for love. It's the end of the search for a person to love. The search for ways to love that person has just begun.

– *Unknown*

6. A marriage is not a noun; it's a verb. It isn't something you get. It's something you do. It's the way you love your partner every day.

– *Barbara De Angelis*

5.   A great marriage is not when the "perfect couple" comes together. It is when an imperfect couple learns to enjoy their differences.

— *Dave Meurer*

4.   Over 50 percent of marriages end in divorce. Many people aren't even getting married to avoid that statistic. I contend that you get out of a marriage what you put into it. Make it a priority to date your wife, to take care of her needs, and grow the bond between you.

— *Josh Hatcher*

3.   Every marriage needs two rooms and one bed.

— *Mantaranjot Mangat, Plotless (2020)*

2.   Marriage is an alliance entered into by a man who can't sleep with the window shut, and a woman who can't sleep with the window open.

— *George Bernard Shaw*

And my number one all-time favorite marriage quote is…

1.   My poor, poor son. Have you not learned? Women don't listen, they talk. Listening is our job. In return, we get sex, children, and food.

— *J.J. McAvoy, The Untouchables (2015)*

Lastly, I'll close out this silly book with one final marriage quote for you to ponder:

> **Love, n. A temporary insanity curable by marriage.**
> – *Ambrose Bierce, The Unabridged Devil's Dictionary (1911)*

LET'S GET CONNECTED

I hope you enjoyed this silly book! If so, **please do two small favors for me right now.**

First, please take a minute to leave a short review of this book on Amazon, Goodreads, or any other website. Online reviews help new readers find this book. Your help in spreading the word about this book is greatly appreciated!

Second, please sign up for my reader's list at www.mikekowis.com/signup/ so that we can get connected. After you join, I'll occasionally share exclusive giveaways and announcements about my upcoming books and speaking engagements.

If you have any questions or wish to contact me about speaking to your group, I'm just an email away! Feel free to contact me anytime at *mike.kowis.esq@gmail.com*.

Happy Trails!

ACKNOWLEDGEMENTS

This book would not have been possible without the extraordinary help and support of many folks, including my dear family, friends, and fellow authors.

I also want to offer my sincere appreciation to my long-time friend and movie aficionado, Robert Ziggy Parker, for his generous help in refining the testimonials for this book. In case you didn't figure it out, I made them up for my readers' amusement. If you didn't enjoy them, I blame Mr. Parker! If you loved them, I want to thank you in advance and let you know that Ziggy played a big part in making these zingers as humorous as possible.

Last, I want to give special thanks to Robynne Alexander at Damonza for the cover design, interior print formatting, and eBook conversion work.

It takes a skillful and dedicated team to create a book like this, and everyone who participated has my sincere appreciation for their contributions.

ABOUT THE AUTHOR

By day, **Mike Kowis, Esq.**, is a mild-mannered tax attorney at a Fortune 500 company in Texas. By night, he swaps a three-piece suit for a pair of tights and a shiny red cape and then begins his duties as a modern-day SUPERHERO (also known as Adjunct Faculty Member) for one of the largest community colleges in the Lone Star State.

Specifically, Mike has practiced corporate tax law for 27 years, including the last quarter-century at Entergy Services, LLC where he currently serves as Senior Tax Counsel. In addition, he has taught corporate tax and business law classes at Lone Star College-Montgomery since 2001. In his spare time, he writes books and competes in off-road races.

Mike holds a bachelor's degree and two law degrees, including a LL.M. in taxation from Georgetown University Law Center. He lives in the piney woods of East Texas with his family and a rambunctious puppy named Mr. Pickles. His eleven nonfiction books are listed below in their order of publication:

1. *Engaging College Students: A Fun and Edgy Guide for Professors* (a college teaching guide with 44 practical tips to engage students in classroom discussions),

2. *14 Steps to Self-Publishing a Book* (a self-publishing guide that has sold over 5,000 copies),

3. ***Maximize Your Book Sales With Data Analysis: The Cure for Authorship Analysis Paralysis*** (a free Kindle eBook for authors written by Sharon C. Jenkins and myself),

4. ***Smart Marketing for Indie Authors: How I Sold my First 1,563 Books and Counting!*** (a book marketing guide for newbie authors),

5. ***Texas Off-road Racing: A Father-Son Journey to a Side-by-Side Championship*** (the true story of off-road racing with my teenage son during our run for the 2019 Championship of a local cross-country series),

6. ***American Tax Triva: The Ultimate Quiz on U.S. Taxation***, (250 fun-filled trivia questions about the fascinating history of U.S. tax law, the IRS, tax forms, and much more),

7. ***Texas Off-road Racing 2: The Battle for ATV and Side-by-Side Championships*** (this sequel shares the gritty details of ATV and side-by-side racing during Mike's run for the 2022 Championships of a new cross-country series),

8. ***The Little Black Book of Tax Wisdom: Quotes, Quips, & Quiddities Every Tax Advisor Should Know*** (a huge collection of amusing tax quotes from Mark Twain, Chris Rock, Ronald Reagan, Winston Churchill, George Washington, Judge Learned Hand, David Letterman, and many more),

9. ***The Little Black Book of Retirement Wisdom: Amusing Quotes for Retirees*** (a riveting collection of humorous and thought-provoking retirement quotes from Betty White, Elon Musk, Mark Twain, Brett Favre, Joan Rivers, Dr. Dre, Billy Graham, George Foreman, and many more),

10. ***The Little Black Book of Birthday Wisdom: Quotes on Aging, Life, and Birthday Cake*** (a fun collection of amusing quotes about aging, life, and birthday cake from Jerry Seinfeld, Abraham Lincoln, Oprah Winfrey, Sylvestor Stallone, Mark Twain, George Burns, Betty White, and many more), and

11. ***The Little Black Book of Marriage Wisdom: Quotes on Weddings, Divorce, & Happily Ever After*** (a large collection of amusing marriage quotes from Ann Landers, Dr. Suess, Zig Ziglar, Jerry Seinfeld, Mark Twain, Oprah Winfrey, and many more).

If you have any questions or would like Mike to speak at an upcoming event, please email him at mike.kowis.esq@gmail.com, find his author page on Facebook (Mike Kowis, Esq.), or visit his website at www.mikekowis.com.

www.ingramcontent.com/pod-product-compliance
Lightning Source LLC
Chambersburg PA
CBHW060511030426
42337CB00015B/1851